YOU CHOOSE
BOOKS

GETTYSBURG BATTLEFIELD

A CHILLING INTERACTIVE ADVENTURE

by Matt Doeden

CAPSTONE PRESS
a capstone imprint

You Choose Books are published by Capstone Press,
1710 Roe Crest Drive, North Mankato, Minnesota 56003
www.mycapstone.com

Library of Congress Cataloging-in-Publication Data
Names: Doeden, Matt, author.
Title: Gettysburg Battlefield : a chilling interactive adventure / by Matt
   Doeden.
Description: North Mankato, Minnesota : Capstone Press, [2017] | Series: You
   choose books. You choose: haunted places | Audience: Ages 8-12. |
   Audience: Grades 4 to 6. | Includes bibliographical references and index.
Identifiers: LCCN 2016035560| ISBN 9781515736493 (library binding) | ISBN
   9781515736547 (ebook (pdf)
Subjects: LCSH: Haunted places—Pennsylvania—Gettysburg—Juvenile
   literature. | Battlefields—Pennsylvania—Gettysburg—Juvenile literature.
   | Gettysburg, Battle of, Gettysburg, Pa., 1863—Juvenile literature. |
   Gettysburg National Military Park (Pa.)—Juvenile literature.
Classification: LCC BF1472.U6 D63 2017 | DDC 133.1/29748/42—dc23
LC record available at https://lccn.loc.gov/2016035560

Editorial Credits
Mari Bolte, editor; Heidi Thompson, designer; Wanda Winch, media researcher;
Gene Bentdahl, production specialist

Photo Credits
Alamy: David Monette, 66; Bridgeman Images: Private Collection/Don Troiani, 100;
CriaImages.com: Jay Robert Nash Collection, 103; Jason R. Butler, Creations by Sole's
Denounce, 20, 29, 32, 88; Library of Congress: Prints and Photographs Division, cover
(bottom), 1 (bottom), 39, 45, 48, 57, 74, 78; Newscom: Stock Connection Worldwide/
Andre Jenny, 18, Zuma Press/Brian Cahn, 81; Shutterstock: Colleen E. Scott/Scott
Designs, 98, Geoffrey Kuchera, 6, 22, happykanppy, background design, Igor Vitkovskiy,
fog design, Jeremy R. Smith Sr., 62, kimshanephotos, 42, Nagel Photography, 4, 9,
Plateresca, paper design, run4it, ink painting background, saki80, frame design, STILLFX,
grey grunge texture, Zack Frank, 13; Thinkstock: Dave Huss, cover (top), 95; [Fighting on
the Ridges] www.gallon.com, 69, [Little Round Top and the Valley of Death] www.gallon.
com, 36

Printed in Canada.
10050S17

TABLE OF CONTENTS

INTRODUCTION

YOU are about to set foot on the grounds of historic Gettysburg. It was the site of the bloodiest battle of the Civil War, and the Union's victory there helped turn the tide of the war. Many believe that restless spirits of soldiers killed during the battle linger on today in the fields and buildings of Gettysburg. The choices you make will drive the story. Will you seek out the long-lost secrets of Gettysburg? Will you relive the terrible battle? And will the experience change you ... forever?

THE BLOODY BATTLEFIELD

"Can you be serious for a second?" you scold your older brother, Peter. He's been horsing around all day, and you're getting tired of it. "Don't you know that this is sacred ground? It's *Gettysburg*, Peter. The bloodiest battle of the Civil War! Two of our great-great grandfathers fought on these fields. One of them *died* here."

Peter shrugs. He knows the stories. But they don't seem to affect him the way they do you. You've always been fascinated with history and genealogy, the stories of your ancestors. And now you're standing on a place where two of them fought, more than a century and a half ago—one for the North, one for the South.

Turn the page.

As you scan the open fields and stands of trees, you can't help wondering if your ancestors could have met. *Of course, they probably wouldn't have known each other,* the reasonable voice in your head tells yourself. But the idea still fills you with wonder.

You've spent the day watching a re-enactment of the great battle. Your grandfather is a certified Civil War buff. He travels around the country, taking part in these re-enactments. You always thought the idea was kind of silly. But you'd also never been to one before.

Now, after having actually seen your grandfather and his friends in action, you've never been more excited about learning more about Gettysburg, the Civil War, and your family's connection to it. You're glad now that your parents made you and Peter come along.

The Gettysburg National Civil War re-enactment takes place every year on the anniversary of the battle.

"So is this what you want to do?" Peter asks. "Wander around some ancient battlefield? Grandpa is going to be hanging out with his friends all night at the campsite talking about the war. That means we can do whatever we want. Let's go into town and catch a movie. There's that new haunted house flick that looks good."

Turn the page.

You sigh. Typical Peter. You came all the way to Gettysburg and he wants to sit in some musty old theater, watching a bad movie. But he's your older brother, and—against your vocal objections—your grandpa put him in charge. Yet you desperately want to stay and explore. You never know when you'll get a chance to come back, and you don't want to waste your time here. You shake your head, amazed that your brother would rather watch fake ghosts on a movie screen than see a piece of history.

Fake ghosts. That gives you an idea. "You know Peter, if it's ghost stories you're after, we should really stick around. People say this place is full of restless spirits that come out after dark. Look, the sun will be setting before long. We could turn this into a ghost hunt."

You can tell he's mulling it over. You don't believe a word of the ghost stories, but it's the type of thing that might captivate Peter. And if you can see the sights while Peter believes you're hunting for ghosts, then you'll happily play along. Yet he still seems unsure.

"Wait!" you say, remembering one of the pamphlets you collected earlier in the day. You dig into your back pocket and find the one marked *Ghosts of Gettysburg*. It shows all of the paranormal hot spots on the grounds. "Check it out, see?"

Peter's eyes light up as he sees the creepy artwork on the page. You can tell he's hooked. "Let's see what we've got here," he says, looking at the map.

Turn the page.

"Ooh, this one's called the Devil's Den!"
Peter exclaims. "Says it's a haunted battlefield.
Or there's an old building where the orphans
of dead soldiers were sent. Betcha that place is
just crawling with ghosts and creepy old stuff.
What do you think? Which one should we check
out first?"

To go to the Devil's Den, go to page 13.

To check out the Soldier's Orphanage,
turn to page 17.

You're here for real Civil War history. The Devil's Den is a good place to start. It was the sight of some major fighting during the battle. As you walk toward the famous site, Peter reads from the pamphlet. "Devil's Den is a large outcropping of rocks. No one knows where its sinister name comes from. Reports of restless spirits there existed even before the Civil War."

Devil's Den is south of the town of Gettysburg.

Turn the page.

"Creepy," you agree, knowing you've got to keep Peter interested.

The sun hangs low in the sky, casting long shadows onto the ground. The den's tall slabs of rock tower up out of uneven ground, almost like a natural fortress. Valleys and crevices between the rocks would make good natural hiding places. Soldiers could regroup before mounting a fresh attack. Flat, open ground surrounds the rocks, giving any watchers a clear view of the territory. You can see why this would have been an important strategic location.

As you stare up at the boulders, something makes you shrink back. You shake your head. *Nothing's there*, you tell yourself. Peter, meanwhile, is already rushing ahead. "Let's get to the top!" he shouts over his shoulder.

The boulders are large, but you could climb them. As you stare up, you notice something … a person? Yes, it's a young man—barely more than a boy. He stands on top of one of the boulders, arms crossed, looking down at you.

You can't make out his features, which are cast into shadow by a big, floppy hat. But as you watch him, he gestures to you, as if inviting you to come up to the top.

"You're not the only one who had that idea," you call out to Peter, pointing toward the boy.

"What are you talking about?" Peter asks.

You turn to look at the boy. But now there's nobody there. You shiver. Was it your imagination? You scoff. Is Peter's silly pamphlet getting to you?

Turn the page.

"Ahh, cool!" Peter whispers. It takes you a moment to realize what he's talking about. But then you see it. A thin layer of fog is rolling in. It's just a few inches high, but it creeps along the ground like a living thing, spreading out and swallowing everything in its path.

"You were right, this place is amazing," Peter says. He starts to climb. "You coming or what?"

To climb the boulders, turn to page 22.

To refuse, turn to page 25.

You'd love to stay here on the battlegrounds. But one glance at the sky tells you that you don't have a lot of daylight left. Maybe it's best to head into town and check out the orphanage. You can always come back in the morning.

Soon you're walking down the streets of Gettysburg. It's a beautiful place, with classic architecture and a real small-town feel. The building that once housed the Soldier's Orphanage stands on Baltimore Street. During the day, it's a bustling street filled with tourists. But now, after sunset, it seems strangely deserted.

"There it is," Peter calls out. He points to a white-and-brick building that bears the words SOLDIER'S NATIONAL MUSEUM on the front. The orphanage closed down soon after the war because of reports of abuse, and was later turned into a museum.

Turn the page.

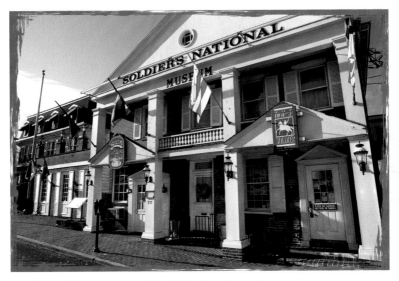

The building that housed the Soldier's National Museum was constructed before the Civil War. It served as a museum for more than 50 years before closing its doors in 2014.

But to your disappointment, the museum is closed. You and Peter stand on the cobbled sidewalk staring at the building, not sure what to do next.

You jump in surprise when an old man calls out to you. You hadn't heard him approach, and his appearance is a shock.

"Nothing to see in there," the man says. "Been shut down for some years now." And, as quickly as he appeared, he's gone.

"That stinks," Peter says. "Let's peek inside, at least." He steps up to the main entrance, cupping his hands over his eyes to peer inside. But before he even touches the door, it cracks open with a bone-chilling *creeeeeeek*!

"Whoa!" Peter stumbles back in surprise.

The building is dark, with no signs of activity. It doesn't look like it's been used in a long time. Yet ... the door just opened!

"Think there's someone in there?" Peter asks.

You peer in through the slit in the open door. It's dark. The air that wafts out smells damp and musty. "I don't think so."

Turn the page.

"Hmm." Peter scratches his head. "Must have been the wind. Let's go in."

A cool breeze blows past you as you step inside the building. As your eyes slowly adjust to the darkness, you feel a poke in the back.

"Cut it out, Peter," you say, annoyed.

"Huh?" You look up. Peter's across the room.

The Soldier's Museum once housed orphans whose fathers were killed in the Civil War.

You whirl around. But there's nothing there. After scanning the room, you know you're definitely alone. You break out into a cold sweat. Your hands start to tremble.

Then you hear laughter. It's a small voice—a child's. And it's distant. It seems to be coming from below you.

"Peter," you whisper. "I don't think we're alone in here."

To go downstairs to investigate the voice, turn to page 27.

To flee the building and return to your grandfather, turn to page 80.

Are your eyes playing tricks on you?
You shake your head and rub your temples.
It must have been your imagination.

Peter's already halfway up the boulder. You
shrug your shoulders and start after him. The
rock feels cool and smooth under your hands.
You confidently scale your way up, finding easy
footholds and handholds along the way.

Confederate snipers used the rocks at Devil's Den for cover
as they shot at Union troops.

Finally, Peter grabs your arm and helps haul you up to the top. Even in the dimming evening light, you can see a long way from here. The fog is still creeping across the ground. Now you can see that it seems to be originating near a creek.

You glance behind you, toward a thick grove. And you notice something that makes your blood run cold. The boy with the floppy hat stands at the edge of the trees, staring right at you. How could that be possible? Only a minute ago, he was standing on top of this very boulder. You can't imagine how he could have traveled down the boulder and to the woods in so little time.

The boy is tall and thin, dressed in patched overalls. But that's not what grabs your attention. It could be the fading light, or the fog, or maybe just your imagination. But you'd swear you can almost see through him.

Turn the page.

Once again, he gestures to you. Then again, he's gone before you can point him out to Peter.

"I swear, there was someone there," you insist. Peter just smirks. You realize he's not listening at all—he's taking a selfie! Then he plops down on the rock, sending it to someone on his phone. He doesn't look like he'll be moving any time soon.

To follow the figure on your own, turn to page 34.

To stay here with Peter, turn to page 36.

"Come on, Peter," you protest. "What's wrong with you? We didn't come out here to climb rocks. Are we going to look around out here or what?"

Peter steps back, away from the boulder. He whirls around and sticks a finger in your chest. "What's wrong with *you*?" he shouts back. "I keep suggesting fun things to do, and all you do is complain and whine. I'm done with it."

With that, Peter turns and begins walking away. "Come back," you plead.

"I'm going to a movie," he barks without even turning around. "You're welcome to join me."

"Grandpa is going to be mad if you leave me here," you call back.

Turn the page.

"Grandpa will barely notice, he's so wrapped up with his re-enactment buddies back at camp. And besides, it's not my fault if you don't come with me. He did put me in charge, after all." Without another word, he marches off. You stand there, staring at him. You can tell from his tone that he's not bluffing.

You look around. The shadows are growing longer by the moment. The fog, so minor a moment ago, is getting thicker. And you can't get the image of that strange boy out of your mind. You're not quite sure if the idea of staying out here alone is exciting or terrifying.

To stay and explore on your own, turn to page 39.

To go with Peter, turn to page 59.

"The sound came from downstairs," Peter says, his voice quivering. He's spooked, but you know he's too proud to admit it. Part of you wants to get out of here, but your curiosity gets the better of you. Together you and Peter creep down the dusty hallway. There's a door leading to a narrow, creaking set of stairs.

It's pitch black at the bottom of the stairs. A dim cone of light from Peter's phone is all you have to see by. Motes of dust swirl and dance in the pale white light as Peter shines it in every direction.

The place is cold and damp. A network of crisscrossing pipes clings to heavy stone walls. A series of long, low wooden benches is neatly arranged along the length of the cellar. The sound of your footsteps echoes off the walls.

Turn the page.

Laughter. You jump. There it is again! It echoes through the cellar in a way that makes it sound like it's coming from every direction at once.

Something brushes against your arm. A cold draft sends shivers down your spine.

"Look at this," Peter whispers.

You step toward him. He's shining his light toward one side of the room. It takes you a moment to realize what you're looking at. Chains are fixed to the walls. At the end of each chain is a small, metal cuff—the kind that might go around a person's wrist.

Your stomach turns. You fear for a moment that you might vomit.

Out of nowhere, an odd thought crosses your mind. For reasons you cannot explain, you feel a powerful urge to touch the chains.

Orphans were chained in the basement.

To touch the chains, turn to page 30.

To continue searching the cellar, turn to page 46.

This is something you have to do. You hesitate for a moment, mentally bracing yourself. Your hand trembles as you slowly reach for the dangling chains. You can feel that something is about to happen, but you can't imagine what.

The moment you touch the chains, a jolt surges through your body. A wave of dizziness overwhelms you. You nearly collapse.

As your senses return, you find yourself in a changed room. Much of it appears cloaked in a mist. There's no sign of Peter. Instead, a small figure sits slumped on a bench. It's a young boy. The chain's cuffs grip his wrists, anchoring him to the wall.

The boy looks up. You recoil in shock.

"Can you help?" the boy asks softly.

"W-who are you?" you stutter. "Why are you here?" Your mind is racing, trying to make sense of what you're seeing.

"I'm Johnny," the child answers. "Rosa punishes us when we're bad. But I'm hungry. Can you help me? Please?"

You take a step forward. At the same moment, the sound of the cellar door opening and footsteps descending echoes through the cellar.

"She's coming," whispers Johnny. "Quick!"

The mists that shroud the room seem to contract. The footsteps thunder louder and louder as the room seems to shrink, the walls closing in tighter. Johnny calls out again, but now his voice seems very far away.

Turn the page.

Your knees buckle. You collapse to the ground, cracking your head on the corner of a bench. The room fades away as darkness creeps in around the edges of your vision.

When the haze clears, the mist is gone. There's no sign of Johnny. There's nothing but a dark room, the light of Peter's phone, and dangling chains.

In 1876 Rosa Carmichael was arrested for abuse against the orphans left in her care. However, her punishment was light and her cruelty continued.

There's no time to rest though. Peter stands over you, pulling you to your feet. "Wake up!" he shouts, panic in his voice. "We have to go!"

At first, you're confused. But then you see the reason for his panic. Small white figures seem to be coming out of all the walls. They're moving toward you, a circle that closes more every moment. You glance from the figures to the chains on the wall. The cuffs that dangle from the nearest chains are closed tight. Johnny's voice echoes in your head.

To open the cuffs, turn to page 89.

To run, turn to page 91.

You have to find out the secret of the ghost boy. "I'll be right back," you tell Peter, scrambling down the opposite side of the boulder. Back on solid ground, the thickening fog is now up to your ankles. Seeing your feet disappear into the mist makes this all feel like a dream.

You hurry to the edge of the wooded area, where you last saw the figure. The woods are cloaked in shadow, and it's hard to make out anything in detail.

You're just about to give up when the ghost appears again, this time deeper within the woods. The sun hangs onto the horizon now, and its light is almost out. Yet you chase the boy anyway.

No matter how fast you move, though, the ghost is always distant. You can never get close enough to get a good look.

Meanwhile, the thick, soupy fog swallows your legs all the way to the shins, and you begin to stumble over the rough ground. But the boy seems to float above the mist.

Finally, the figure stops in a small clearing near a small creek. For the first time, he allows you to get close. Twenty feet … ten. Your whole body tingles. You can feel your hair standing up, as if from static electricity. The temperature here feels 20 degrees colder.

The figure points at the ground. Then he disappears.

In the distance, you hear Peter's voice, shouting your name. It sounds urgent.

To find Peter, turn to page 52.

To investigate the area where the ghost pointed, turn to page 55.

You're not ready to go chasing after mystery figures on your own. With a sigh, you plop down next to Peter. While he types away, you just take in the scenery. If you ignore the monuments, it's hard to imagine that one of history's bloodiest battles was fought here. The rolling hills, woods, and fields all seem so quiet and peaceful now.

Electronic devices failing, sounds of ghostly battles, and apparitions of deceased soldiers are commonly reported at Gettysburg.

As you scan the scenery, something catches your eye. In the distance, you spot a strange blue light. It's an orb, and it seems to be hovering above the ground, bobbing through the trees.

"What's that?" you ask, elbowing Peter in the ribs. He grunts and looks up.

"Don't see anything." His distracted gaze returns to his phone.

You jab him harder and point to the spot. "There," you whisper.

Peter squints. "Somebody with a flashlight?"

"No way. It's not a flashlight."

"Trick of the sunlight? Reflection off of something?" Peter goes on, trying to explain it. But you can tell he's stumped.

Turn the page.

The pale blue orb continues to hover and dance, right along a tree-covered ridge. You guess it's less than half a mile from where you sit.

Peter sticks his phone in his pocket. "Okay, you've got me curious. Let's go check it out."

The two of you take off toward the light. It hovers just beyond a stand of trees, dipping and bobbing around in an almost hypnotic pattern.

"What is that?" Peter whispers. The two of you move closer. The orb is the size of a basketball, maybe a bit smaller. It seems to be made of pure light, rather than anything solid. In one of its seemingly random movements, it dips—right toward you!

To reach out to the orb, turn to page 43.

To dodge out of its way, turn to page 71.

You watch as Peter marches away. Even after he's gone, you find yourself staring in that direction, half expecting him to come back. But he doesn't. You're on your own.

"Good," you mutter to yourself. Now you can do what you want and go where you want. But the sun is starting to set, casting shades of deep orange and red. It's pretty, but soon there will be no light at all. Was this really such a good idea?

Fighting at Devil's Den took place on the second day of battle. At least 100,000 soldiers took part, and around 20,000 of those were killed, wounded, captured, or were among the missing.

Turn the page.

But after what you said to Peter, you can't go back right away. You've still got time to visit a few spots. The Devil's Den is close to a few other major landmarks. One of them is Little Round Top, one of the most famous landmarks of the battle. Another is Cemetery Ridge, where the South made a last, desperate charge into the Union line on the last day of fighting.

To make your way toward Little Round Top, go to page 41.

To head toward Cemetery Ridge, turn to page 48.

You head out in the direction of Little Round Top, a rocky hill that was the center of a lot of the fighting at Gettysburg. Along the way, you stop to look at several Union monuments. You're surprised by how deserted the place is, even this late. During the day, it was crawling with visitors. Now you feel as though you're the only one in the nearly 6,000 acres of Gettysburg National Military Park.

The evening is cool, and the quiet stillness is almost eerie.

Pop! Pop! Sharp noises shatter the silence. It sounds like rifle fire. You whirl around, spotting two small groups of men across a field, near a stand of trees. Then there's the sound of another shot. Then another.

Turn the page.

Huh? Your grandpa said the fighting part of the re-enactment was done for the day. Why are they doing this now, and with nobody around to watch?

To find out what's going on, turn to page 50.

To continue on to Little Round Top, turn to page 62.

The second day of fighting at Gettysburg ranks as the 10th bloodiest battle overall of the Civil War.

The air around you seems to crackle with electricity. You can feel the hairs on your arm and neck standing up. As the strange blue spirit orb swoops silently toward you, you reach for it.

As you connect, a shock ripples through your body. It's not painful, but the power surge knocks you over and blinds you for a moment.

As your vision clears, you find yourself confused and disoriented. This place is familiar ... but not. It's mid-day now. The smell of smoke hangs in the air. The loud rumble of distant cannon fire shakes the ground.

"On your feet, soldier!" A young man in a blue uniform steps over you, staring down. His face is covered in blood and dirt. The past few days have taught you enough to know that the man is dressed as an officer. But his uniform doesn't look quite like what you've seen from the other re-enactors.

Turn the page.

How long have you been asleep? How long has this re-enactment been going on? Nothing makes any sense.

You look down at yourself. You seem to be wearing the blue uniform of a soldier. What in the world?

"Get up!" the officer repeats. Confused and a bit dizzy, you stand. You start to wander away, your head in a haze of confusion. The officer isn't having it. "Your rifle, soldier! Get it together!" he yells.

You turn. Another man dressed in Union blue thrusts a long-barreled gun into your hands. As you stand there, dumbfounded, more blue-clad soldiers emerge out of the woods. Their uniforms are tattered, and their thin, bearded faces are streaked with dirt, soot, and blood.

Although Big Round Top was a higher location, Little Round Top was cleared of trees so it was ideal for attack and defense.

"With me, soldiers," the officer barks. "The enemy is beyond this ridge. Charge!"

Your hands shake. Your head spins. But finally, the situation becomes impossibly clear. This is no re-enactment. This is the Battle of Gettysburg, and you're in the middle of it.

To charge into battle, turn to page 74.

To run away into the woods, turn to page 78.

You shake your head, as if trying to drive the idea out of it. There's absolutely no way you're touching those chains. Something about them feels sinister.

You shiver, and not just from fear—the temperature seems to have dropped 30 degrees all of a sudden. You can see your own breath. As you back away, you feel a presence directly behind you.

Slowly, you turn around. A figure emerges before you. It's in the shape of a young boy. He's pale and thin. You can see right through him as he stares up at you. Your heart races. What you're seeing makes you afraid—but the ghost itself seems harmless.

From the gasp behind you, you know Peter sees it too. Part of you is relieved. At least you're not going insane.

The boy slowly raises a finger to his lips. Then he leans forward. You lean forward too. His whisper is faint. It sounds more like the wind. But the words are crystal clear.

"Rosa's coming. Hide."

In that instant, the door to the cellar staircase flies open. The sound of footsteps echoes down from above. And in that moment, you sense another presence. But this one is evil.

To search for someplace to hide, turn to page 83.

To stand your ground, turn to page 86.

The second day of fighting took place at Devil's Den, Little Round Top, Seminary Ridge, Oak Ridge, Barlow's Knoll, Oak Hill, and around the town of Gettysburg.

You've listened to your grandfather enough to know about Cemetery Ridge. This is where the heaviest fighting took place. It's also the spot where one of your ancestors was killed.

The sun drops more toward the horizon with each step you take. You can almost imagine the battle here among the grassy slopes littered with piles of rocks. This is where the Confederate army focused their largest charge.

You approach a stand of hickory trees.
To your surprise, there's a figure dressed in Union blue standing in front of the trees. It must be one of the re-enactors, you decide after a moment of hesitation. Perhaps he's preparing for a re-enactment of Pickett's Charge tomorrow.

As you stare, the man turns in your direction. He's far enough away that you can't make out any features. But he raises his arm and waves it frantically in your direction. One of the buttons on his jacket catches the sunlight, reflecting brightly back at you.

What does he want? Is he waving you over? Or could he be waving you away?

To go to the man, turn to page 93.

To continue along the ridge toward Cemetery Hill, turn to page 97.

You move in the direction of the action. About twenty soldiers, all dressed in Union blue, pursue half as many men in tattered Confederate gray. Their movements take them behind a thick stand of trees, which blocks your view of the scene for several moments. You wait for the soldiers to emerge from the other side of the trees. But seconds pass. Then a minute. Nothing.

You quicken your pace, running to the spot.

There's nothing here. Nobody. No footprints. Just … nothing. How is that possible? How is any of this possible?

You spin around in a full circle, scanning the landscape. The sun, almost sitting on the horizon, casts long shadows over the ground. But there's still enough light to see by, and nowhere for a group that large to hide. And why would they?

You stand there, dumbfounded, staring toward the stand of trees. Suddenly, a man dressed in a mud-streaked gray uniform runs out from the shadows. BOOM! The rifle fire sounds. Crying out in pain, the man stumbles forward. He twists as he falls, as though a shot clipped him in the shoulder.

That's not what the re-enactment looked like, you think, shuddering. The man lies on the ground, groaning, not 30 feet from you. He looks up, brown eyes becoming more unfocused as the moment goes by. He reaches a trembling hand in your direction.

To rush to the man, turn to page 65.

To turn and run back to your grandpa's campsite, turn to page 69.

You stand there staring at a bare patch of ground. Alone. As the sun sets, you feel a wave of anxiety. What were you thinking, wandering off to chase a ghost? You try to get your bearings, but the fog makes it difficult. Everything looks the same. You reach down, grab a fallen tree branch, and plant it in the ground, hopeful that you'll be able to find the spot again. Then, with a hint of regret and even sadness, you turn and move back in the direction of Peter's voice.

"PETER!" you shout. "I'M ON MY WAY!"

For several minutes, the two of you shout back and forth as you move over the fog-covered ground. The sun has set now, and finding your way through the shadowy twilight proves more difficult than you'd guessed. By the time you finally find Peter, it's fully dark.

Peter is furious. "You can't run off like that!" he scolds. You can hear in his voice that he was really afraid. "What were you thinking?"

You explain it all, expecting him to laugh in your face. But he doesn't. Maybe it's the tone of your voice. Maybe it's his desire to believe. But he doesn't doubt your story for a moment.

"We'll come back here," he promises. "But first, we need to find Grandpa."

First thing the next morning, you and Peter drag your grandfather out to the site.

"Tell me again what we're looking for," your grandfather says with a sigh. He's a patient man, but you can tell he thinks both of you have gone nuts. And it's hard to blame him—you honestly don't know how to answer the question. What *are* you looking for?

Turn the page.

You search for almost two hours. Nothing looks familiar. Defeated, you finally agree to head back. The next re-enactment is about to start, and your grandfather doesn't want to be late. You vow to come back and search again, to solve this mystery. But deep down, you know that you probably missed your chance. And you're sure that not knowing is going to eat at you for the rest of your life.

THE END

To follow another path, turn to page 12.
To learn more about the Gettysburg Battlefield, turn to page 101.

"This way," you shout back to Peter. After what you've just seen, there's no way you're leaving without checking this out first. Odds are you'll never find this exact spot again, and you have the feeling the ghost won't be back to show you the way.

Amazingly, the fog does not cover the ground here. It's all around, like a cloak lying over the entire battlefield, but it's as if something is driving it away where you stand. You drop down on your hands and knees, scraping through the rocky earth with your fingers.

What are you looking for? You can't even guess. But the apparition's message was clear: He wanted you to find something. Minutes pass. Your fingers, now streaked with mud, begin to bleed, but you keep digging.

Turn the page.

Then you hit something smooth. At first, you think it's just rock. But no … it's lighter, not as dense. With every minute that passes, the daylight fades. You barely have enough light left to see what you've found. But as you brush more dirt away, there's no mistaking it. With a sharp breath, you recoil, stumbling backward into the dirt. Your heart races as you regain your nerve and lean back in.

It's a bone. And it looks human.

"PETER!" you shout at the top of your lungs. "PETER!"

Moments later, your brother is there. At first, he's angry with you. But his anger fades away quickly when he realizes what you've found. The two of you stand there together, looking down in awe at your discovery.

"Someone died here. A soldier, maybe," you say. "I think … I think I was supposed to find this. I was brought here to find it."

Peter dials the local police on his phone. It takes nearly an hour, but they eventually find you. The next day, a forensics team comes out to investigate the discovery. What they learn chills you to the bone.

Skirmishes started outside of Gettysburg in the early morning of July 1, 1863. The sounds of fighting attracted other soldiers, and by noon it was a full-blown battle.

Turn the page.

"The remains appear to date from the time of the battle," the forensic scientist in charge of the investigation tells you. "They belonged to a young male, probably around 16 years old. He's been here, undiscovered, all this time. The park will be putting a marker here to honor what must have been a fallen soldier. How on earth did you find this?"

You have no way to answer that question. Who would believe it? But you know, and you believe that you've helped a restless spirit find some peace. You can't help but smile.

THE END

To follow another path, turn to page 12.
To learn more about the Gettysburg Battlefield, turn to page 101.

You're torn. As badly as you want to stay and explore, you're not sure you want to do it alone. And you don't want to get in trouble. Your grandfather is a patient and forgiving man. Running off on your own in the middle of a huge national park, in the middle of the night, though, would probably be enough to set off his temper.

"Just a sec," you beg. As your brother waits impatiently, you take your phone out and snap a quick picture of Devil's Den. Who knows if you'll ever see it again? Then with a heavy sigh, you follow Peter.

An hour later, you're sitting in a movie theater, ready to watch the latest ghost movie start to roll. You've got popcorn, soda, and a comfy seat right in the center.

Turn the page.

As other people shuffle in, you play idly with your phone. The picture you took of Devil's Den looks great as your phone's wallpaper. As the lights go down, you move to turn your phone off. The second before the screen goes blank, something catches your eye. But then it goes black, and whatever you thought you saw is gone.

Uneasy, you focus on the movie. It's not bad, and actually helps settle you down. It's got a couple of scenes that actually make you scream out loud. And though you'd never admit it, just spending time with your big brother is nice.

Halfway through, Peter gets up to go to the bathroom. You let him by, and then focus back on the big screen. But even though your brother is gone, you get the sense that someone is sitting next to you. The smell of gunpowder fills the air. Then your pocket begins to vibrate.

You pull your phone out. The screen is glowing. A silvery mist seems to rise from it. Slowly it takes form—it's the boy you saw at the battlefield. He stares right at you, points his finger, and …

When Peter returns, you're nowhere to be found. None of the other theatergoers saw anything. The police are baffled. The only thing they ever find is your phone—with a huge crack down the middle of the screen.

THE END

To follow another path, turn to page 12.
To learn more about the Gettysburg Battlefield, turn to page 101.

The noises are odd. But Little Round Top is ahead, and you've seen enough re-enacting for one day. With a shrug, you continue on your way.

Little Round Top rises above the fields of Gettysburg, overshadowed only by its rocky neighbor, Big Round Top. As you approach, you can see the silhouette of the statue of Union officer Gouverneur K. Warren.

Union General Gouverneur Kemble Warren realized that Little Round Top would be an important location during the battle. He sent soldiers to hold down the area right before fighting began.

Eager to get a closer look, you start to scramble up the hill, rather than find a path. Loose stone and rock make the climb difficult. About halfway up the hill, on one of the steeper parts of the climb, something tugs on your ankle. Your foot slips.

Frantically you reach out with a hand, grabbing for anything. Too late—your ankle buckles under you with a sickening pop. You slide down the hill, fingers reaching for a hold. But every time you make contact with something, your grip seems to loosen, sending you tumbling again. You hit the ground hard. Your ankle twists and snaps, sending waves of pain up your leg.

You groan in agony. The noise echoes back at you, a stark reminder that you're all alone out here. One glance down tells you all you need to know. Your ankle is broken.

Turn the page.

"Help!" you shout out into the night. Something that sounds a bit like a laugh echoes back at you. Then it's gone. No one can hear you. "Help!" you shout again and again.

No one answers your call. You have no hope of making it down on your own. So you're stuck, at the mercy of other visitors and Mother Nature.

It's a long night filled with chills and pain. You drift in and out of consciousness. At one point, what looks like a Union soldier stands over you. A dream? A hallucination? You can't even be sure.

Just make it until morning, you remind yourself. *Help will come.* But even if you have what it takes to hold on that long, there's no guarantee anyone will make it in time to find you.

THE END

To follow another path, turn to page 12.
To learn more about the Gettysburg Battlefield, turn to page 101.

Is the man really hurt? You have to help, if you can. Setting your fears aside, you rush to his side.

You kneel down and look at the man. Then you nearly topple over in shock. For a fleeting instant, you're certain that it's your grandfather lying here before you. The man's face, streaked with blood and sweat, looks so familiar. But he's young—probably no older than twenty-five. It can't be him.

The soldier's left shoulder is soaked in dark red blood. He breathes in short, shallow gasps. His eyes meet yours, and an intense wave of energy seems to pass between you. His eyes grow wide, as if in shock. You reach down to grab his arm, but your hand passes right through it.

This is a ghost, you finally admit to yourself. It's either that or you've gone insane.

Turn the page.

Then the weight of it hits you. This isn't just any ghost. This has to be the ghost of your great-great grandfather. The moment the idea occurs to you, there is no doubt about it. For reasons you cannot begin to explain, you're being shown his death. And stranger still, he seems aware of you. He doesn't speak a word, but you can see it in his eyes. He knows. It seems impossible, but he knows.

Field hospitals were set up in any available building with water nearby. Army doctors would treat sick or wounded soldiers as they arrived from the battlefield.

Your mind races. You're desperate to help, to somehow save his life. But your hands pass right through him. You can't even try to stop the bleeding. You're completely helpless.

Fortunately the end comes quickly. You stay with him in his final moments, until he breathes his last. As he passes, he seems at peace, making eye contact with you one final time and even smiling a little. You can't help but feel that your presence here is part of the reason. As illogical as it all sounds, you're certain of it.

Once he's truly gone, his form simply fades away, leaving no trace he was ever there. You remain there for several minutes more, weeping over what you just witnessed.

Turn the page.

You cannot explain it. It's not possible. Part of you wants to rush back and tell your grandfather every detail. But another part wants this to remain private, a moment between you and an ancestor that you should never have met.

The sun has completely set by the time you collect yourself and get to your feet. It's time to find your grandpa—now, before it's too late.

THE END

To follow another path, turn to page 12.
To learn more about the Gettysburg Battlefield, turn to page 101.

The first day of fighting came with heavy Confederate losses.

Your gaze lingers a moment longer on the scene across the open field. The more you stare, the more certain you are: *That's not real.* You're either losing your mind, or the spirits of Gettysburg are rising up all around you. You desperately wish Peter was still here. You wish anyone was here. At least if someone else was seeing the same things you are, you'd know you're not crazy.

Turn the page.

But there's nobody. Just you. The fields of Gettysburg grow darker by the moment. A thin fog creeps out over the battlefield. And now this. *No more*, you decide. You turn and dash from the scene, back in the direction of your camp. You run as fast as your feet can carry you over the hallowed ground of Gettysburg, not slowing down until you see the smoke from several dozen campfires rise above the trees ahead. You're heading straight for your grandpa's tent, and you're not looking back. Your time exploring Gettysburg is over.

THE END

To follow another path, turn to page 12.
To learn more about the Gettysburg Battlefield, turn to page 101.

You don't even have time to think. All you can do is react. An instant before contact, you dive to the ground. You can feel the light as it passes over you, a cold electricity crackling in its wake. The orb sings with an eerie high-pitched whine, whizzing past your ear again. It misses you by mere inches. Then, to your horror, it circles around and slams right into Peter!

Peter is thrown off his feet. His body is carried several feet through the air before he crashes hard into the brush. He doesn't make a sound—not a scream, shout, or even a whimper. You rush to his side. His eyes are wide open and he's breathing, but he doesn't respond to anything you say. Even slapping him across the face doesn't seem to break him out of whatever spell he's under.

Turn the page.

"HELP!" you shout out into the night. "ANYONE! HELP!"

Nobody's out here. You find Peter's phone, but it was crushed by the impact. Peter's too heavy for you to carry, but you know he's in desperate need of help. You don't have any choice—you have to leave him here.

"I'll be right back, Peter. Hold on," you promise. With that, you take off at a sprint. Your sense of direction is good. After just a few minutes, you reach a road and flag down an elderly couple on their way out of the park. You call 911 on their phone. Help is there in minutes.

Physically, Peter is all right. He has some scratches and bruises from the fall. But the same isn't true of his mind. His gaze is vacant. Sometimes he speaks, but it's in strange, old-fashioned English, with an Eastern accent.

Doctors are at a loss. They'll keep working with Peter, trying to bring your brother back. You find your thoughts turning back to the battlefield of Gettysburg. What was that blue orb? What did it do to your brother? If it took him away, is there any way it could bring him back? You vow that one day, you'll return to find out.

THE END

To follow another path, turn to page 12.
To learn more about the Gettysburg Battlefield, turn to page 101.

Little Round Top stands at 650 feet (198 meters) above sea level at its highest point.

It's a strange feeling of déjà vu. You're you, but at the same time, you feel like you're someone else. You definitely think you have been here before, but this is your first time to Gettysburg. Even the men feel familiar, as if you knew them long, long ago.

With every moment you spend in this strange flashback reality, things begin to make more and more sense. Memories you shouldn't even have come rushing back. Faces, names. It feels like a flood washing over you, drowning out who you are—or, at least, the person you used to be.

Your head swimming, you have no choice but to follow orders, charging into battle with your rifle in your hands. As you come over the ridge, you see the clashing armies. Soldiers, horses, and cannons seem to be everywhere. A haze of smoke hangs over it all.

Without even thinking about it—without even really knowing how to do it—you raise your rifle and fire toward a line of gray-clad Confederate troops.

Turn the page.

Later on, you remember almost nothing of that terrible day, or the ones that immediately follow. Your reality, the one full of modern memories, slowly fades. The war becomes your new timeline.

Once in a while you get a flash of memory, or a dream you can barely remember, of people and things that don't—can't—exist in the late 1800s. You often wonder if you're crazy.

The war drags on. You fight bravely for the Union, enduring the hardships of war. You're there when Confederate General Robert E. Lee surrenders. After the war, you seem to live in a daze, not really knowing what you're supposed to do next.

Twenty years after the war is over, you return to Gettysburg, to the same stand of trees. And there it hangs—the pale blue orb.

Although you're sure you've never seen it before, it seems to call to you. You step forward and reach out a trembling hand to touch it. The jolt of electricity knocks you to the ground.

"Whoa," you hear. It's ... a voice you know from somewhere. "That was crazy! You okay?"

You stare up, flat on your back. You know that face. It takes a few seconds before you can manage a whisper. "Peter?"

"Let's get you back," says your brother. "Enough adventure for one night."

You struggle to your feet. Enough for one night? That was enough for a lifetime!

THE END

To follow another path, turn to page 12.
To learn more about the Gettysburg Battlefield, turn to page 101.

Everything around you seems to exist in a haze. Your ears ring. Your head swims. Your body feels weak and exhausted. Yet one thought is clear: *This is real.*

You know nothing about a real battle. You don't even know how to fire your weapon. There's no way you're charging into anything right now. Instead, you drop the weapon, turn, and dash into the woods.

The average soldier was around 26 years old. However, near the end of the war, old and young men were pressed into service to replace the soldiers who had been killed in battle.

Your steps feel slow and labored. Heavy boots weigh you down. Every stick and branch seems like it's reaching out to trip you up. You don't make it 20 feet before someone shouts, "Deserter!"

The boom of gunfire rings out. You hear the shot before you feel it, but when you do, the pain is intense. You hit the ground hard, face first. Blood gushes from a wound in your chest, spilling onto the ground. As you breathe your last, your spirit rises up out of your body as a dimly glowing ball of pale blue light.

THE END

To follow another path, turn to page 12.
To learn more about the Gettysburg Battlefield, turn to page 101.

That's it. You're done.

"I don't like this, Peter," you say. "I'm leaving."

"Oh, come on, let's just stay for a few minutes," Peter begs. "Don't get spooked. It's just an old building." He takes a few steps away from you.

But your mind is made up. You're in no mood for a supernatural adventure, especially in a creepy, musty old building. You start to back out, hoping Peter will follow.

He doesn't. And, despite everything you've said, you can't leave him. Timidly, you follow him around the room as he checks out the displays.

"Peter," you whisper. "There's a man in the corner."

"Sure," Peter scoffs.

"No, seriously," you say. "Look, please!" Peter looks up and sees what you see. There, in the corner of the room, is a man in a blue uniform. He has a gray beard and piercing blue eyes. But your eyes can't seem to fully focus on him—he's blurry everywhere, especially near his feet. He moves toward you, faster and faster, before lunging.

There are many interactive museums in Gettysburg that history lovers can visit.

Turn the page.

You and Peter scream and cower as he leaps at you. There's a mighty *whoosh*ing noise and a burst of freezing cold air hits you. But when you look up, the blurry man is gone. The cold air dissipates and you're alone in the museum once again.

It's a race to see who can get out of the museum first. Then it's a race back to the battle site. You barricade yourselves in your tent, and refuse to talk to anyone—especially to anyone wearing a Union blue uniform.

THE END

To follow another path, turn to page 12.
To learn more about the Gettysburg Battlefield, turn to page 101.

You can't begin to imagine what's coming down those steps. And you have no intention of standing here in the open to find out.

"Hide!" you whisper to Peter. Your pulse races as you look for somewhere to hide. CLOMP … CLOMP … CLOMP come the footsteps.

Panic grips you. Where can you go?

"There!" Peter whispers, pointing to the long wooden benches. You dive beneath one of them, lying as flat and as still as you can. The sound of your heartbeat thunders in your eardrums.

The footsteps stop. The already chilly room grows colder still.

A voice rings out. It's like nothing you've ever heard. It's rough and tinny, and seems to echo like it's far away.

"Has someone been misbehaving?"

Turn the page.

CLOMP … CLOMP … CLOMP!

The footsteps are coming in your direction. Every muscle in your body tenses. You choke back a scream.

Suddenly the bench above you is ripped away, tossed against a wall with such violent force that it shatters into pieces. A bony hand grips your ankle, holding you in place.

"NO!" Peter shouts, charging out toward the spirit. Distracted, the ghost's grasp on your ankle weakens. You pull your foot free and scramble to your feet.

"Naughty children!" shrieks the ghost—the pale image of a woman with a flowing dress. The ghost slowly moves toward you. The stench of death and decay overwhelms your senses.

Together, you and Peter dash for the stairs. The ghost lunges toward you, but you're too fast.

You bound up the steps and out into the night, gasping for air. You don't stop running until you're blocks away.

When you stop to catch your breath, you bend down and reach for your ankle. The skin feels clammy and sore. You roll up your pant leg for a better look.

Peter gasps.

The pale blue mark of a hand is burned onto your skin. The finger marks are long and skeletal. The skin where it touched you is cold to the touch. Over the next few days, you wait for the mark to fade—but it never does. It remains a constant reminder of your brush with the paranormal.

THE END

To follow another path, turn to page 12.
To learn more about the Gettysburg Battlefield, turn to page 101.

Peter grabs your hand. Neither of you can look away from the stairway. *CLOMP ... CLOMP ... CLOMP.*

A figure, pale white and wearing a tattered dress, descends. Her face is cloaked in shadow—all except her eyes, which are deep, dark pits. She sends off an aura of pure darkness. "Children!" the ghost shrieks. "Naughty children!"

The ghost—*Rosa*, you remind yourself grimly—hisses, "Back to your chains!" She points a sharp, bony finger toward you. "Naughty children must be punished!"

You think back to the ghost boy, chained forever in this cellar. You feel a wave of rage. The anger wells up inside of you. You grab Peter's phone and lift it up, shining its light directly at the spirit's face. Rosa reels back into the wall with a hideous shriek that makes your blood run cold.

You don't stop. You march forward, right toward the ghost, holding the light before you like a flame. The ghost throws an arm up to guard her face. She begins to fade, as if the light itself is banishing her from the real world.

Just before she disappears, Rosa drops her arm and looks right at you. There is a twisted smile on her face that chills you to the bone. You find yourself staring at the empty space where she stood, unable to get that smile out of your mind.

What did it mean? What did she know?

You're not sticking around to find out. You grab Peter by the arm and bound up the stairs, three at a time. But at the top of the stairs, the old man you saw before is waiting.

"I told you, there nothing in there for you," he repeats, shaking his head sadly. He fades away.

Turn the page.

The Soldier's Museum had a replica dungeon, with a wax doll chained to the wall.

The man is replaced by a small band of teenage boys. A feeling of menace radiates from these new ghosts. Then you see that they are armed with heavy sticks. You cry out as they hit you and Peter. The ghost boys drive you back into the cellar—and back to Rosa.

THE END

To follow another path, turn to page 12.
To learn more about the Gettysburg Battlefield, turn to page 101.

The ghostly figures are filling the room. The temperature seems to drop every time a new ghost enters. They seem to be everywhere. Their whispers tickle in your ear. Peter is begging to leave. But your mind remains fixed on Johnny. You grab the chains on the wall. You pull as hard as you can, fighting against the rusted metal. Snap! One cuff snaps open. Snap! The other!

Your mission complete, you drop the chains and turn to run. But then you notice that the ghosts are gone, and the room is warm again. The cellar is again just a cellar. Your rapid breathing—and Peter's—is the only sound you can hear.

Yet you're not alone. A presence lingers behind you. A pale white mist hovers above the spot where the chains are fixed to the wall. It hangs there for a long moment, as if looking at you. Then it gradually fades away.

Turn the page.

"Good luck to you, Johnny," you whisper.

"What are you talking about?" Peter gasps. "What the heck just happened?"

You take a long, deep breath. You close your eyes and smile. Then you pat your brother on the back.

"We've got a lot to talk about," you tell him. "But first, let's get out of here."

THE END

To follow another path, turn to page 12.
To learn more about the Gettysburg Battlefield, turn to page 101.

The figures are everywhere. They swirl around the room, lingering just out of reach. You grab Peter by the arm and run for the stairs.

Peter doesn't protest. He's every bit as scared as you are. Together, you bound up the stairs, out into the hallway of the ground floor, then out the door into the crisp night air. Together, you collapse on the sidewalk, gasping for breath.

After a few moments, you look at each other. "Did that just happen?" Peter asks.

All you can do is nod. If you'd been alone, you might convince yourself it was a hallucination. But both of you saw it.

For a few days, you can't get the terror out of your mind. But in time, that fades. What remains is the vision of Johnny.

Turn the page.

Guilt eats at you. He asked you for help, and you did nothing. He was already dead, you tell yourself. But that only makes you feel worse, thinking about Johnny suffering for eternity.

Your thoughts often turn back to that abandoned cellar. *I'll go back someday*, you vow. *And next time, I won't let him down.*

THE END

To follow another path, turn to page 12.
To learn more about the Gettysburg Battlefield, turn to page 101.

As you watch, the man waves again. He's clearly trying to get your attention. What does he want? There's only one way to find out.

You head toward him. You can't make out his face, but his uniform is Union blue. A large slash has left the fabric torn from shoulder to navel. It hardly seems like the uniform a re-enactor would wear.

You quicken your pace, but before you can reach him, the man disappears into the trees. The sun has set. Only a glow of orange twilight remains in the sky. The woods are very dark. With a deep breath, you step into the darkness.

The silence here is eerie. With every step you take, sticks crunch under your foot. But no birds are singing, no insects buzzing. No wind rustles the treetops. You're alone in the silence.

Turn the page.

Deeper into the woods you go. For a while, you catch an occasional glance of the man. But then ... nothing. You stop, standing perfectly still in the silent wood, hoping he'll show himself again. Even though everything is deathly silent, you can feel a presence.

But he doesn't appear. Fear begins to well up inside your chest. You take a few careful steps, unsure what to do. You gasp as you almost trip over something in the dark.

You kneel down to inspect what you tripped over. The feeling of someone standing over your shoulder gets stronger, but when you look back no one is there. Your hand falls on a piece of tattered cloth, half-buried in the earth. You carefully dig and work it loose. As you hold it up, a chill runs down your spine.

Union uniforms included a blue wool coat and pants, leather shoes, and a blue forage cap.

It's the jacket of a uniform. The material is badly worn and faded. You can't even tell the color through the layers of mud and grime that cover it. But one feature is crystal clear. The uniform has been torn—or sliced—from one shoulder to the navel.

Turn the page.

You place the uniform back on the ground, then bury it in a shallow grave. As you stand, you realize that the presence you felt before is gone. You're truly by yourself now. And you realize that you really don't want to be alone anymore. It's time to go find your grandpa.

THE END

To follow another path, turn to page 12.
To learn more about the Gettysburg Battlefield, turn to page 101.

You shrug and continue on your way. It seems like Gettysburg keeps coming up with new and interesting mysteries to explore. But you're just not interested in exploring any of them. You'd rather see some statues and hills than investigate the unexplained and unusual.

So that's what you do. As the sun sets over Gettysburg, you wander Cemetery Ridge, imagining the three-day battle that raged here so many years ago. You trace the line of Pickett's Charge and imagine the lines of cannon and cavalry that awaited those Confederate troops. More than 165,000 troops fought here, in a town of 2,400 people. It must have seemed overwhelming to the people who lived there. You can almost imagine field hospitals scattered all over the grounds, filled with wounded.

Turn the page.

Gettysburg's thin soil and rocky ground made digging trenches to hide in difficult. Instead, both sides built stone walls to hide behind.

There's the stone wall where Union troops crouched during the charge, you think. As you climb over the low wall, the smell of gunpowder fills your nose, causing you to sneeze. When you open your eyes, the air has changed. Everything is hazy. The loud boom of artillery shakes the wall.

You can see thousands of Confederate troops advancing over the open ground ahead of you. As you squint for a better look, one of the troops raises his rifle and takes aim. Then he fires. Something both blazing hot and freezing cold hits you in the chest. You collapse.

They find you the next day, at the base of the wall. The coroner has no idea what caused your death. The only thing unusual she can find is a small, bluish mark on your chest that looks like it was caused by a bullet—but there's no hole.

THE END

To follow another path, turn to page 12.
To learn more about the Gettysburg Battlefield, turn to page 101.

EPILOGUE: GHOSTS OF THE PAST

Gettysburg sits in southern Pennsylvania, near the state's border with Maryland. The small farming community that surrounds it is mostly quiet and peaceful. A visitor might never guess that the area has a terrible and bloody past, or that ghosts of that past may linger on today.

In the summer of 1863, at the peak of the Civil War, the armies of the Union and the Confederacy converged on the hills, woods, and open fields of Gettysburg. Confederate General Robert E. Lee had just led his troops to victory in major battles over the Union. Confident, Lee pressed his army north, into enemy territory. The Union troops pursued.

The armies clashed early on July 1. Over three days, the battle sprawled over the fields and ridges. Reinforcements continued to arrive, with more than 165,000 soldiers on the field at the height of battle. Fighting took place around Little Round Top, Cemetery Ridge, Culp's Hill, and across the hills and ridges of Gettysburg.

On July 3 Lee ordered a massive assault. Major General George Pickett led 12,000 to 14,000 Confederate troops into the heart of the Union line. But the bold maneuver, known as Pickett's Charge, failed, as the Union army's artillery and firepower won out.

In total, as many as 51,000 men were killed, captured, or went missing on the field of battle. It was the most casualties in any American battle in history. Legend tells that the streets of Gettysburg ran red with blood.

Confederate troops had to travel nearly a mile across an open field during Pickett's Charge.

The Union victory came at a great cost. But it also marked a turning point in the war. Lee was forced into a retreat from which the Confederates never recovered. The Union generals drove the Confederates from the Northern states, then pursued them deep into the heart of the South.

Two years later, Lee surrendered at Appomattox Court House in Virginia. The Confederacy was dead. The Union had won.

The war was over, but the scars on Gettysburg remained. More than a century and a half after the battle was fought, echoes of the past still linger. Gettysburg National Military Park now stands where much of the fighting took place. Visitors can walk in the shadow of the bloody battle. Many who do are filled with a sense of awe. Some seem to sense something more.

Strange sights and sounds lead many to believe Gettysburg is haunted by restless war-torn spirits. Visitors hear the shouting of soldiers and the distant sound of cannon fire. They report seeing strange figures, floating lights, and mysterious fog.

From the young man with the floppy hat who roams Devil's Den to a ghost dog who seems to guard his master's grave the reports are everywhere.

Even the Soldier's Orphanage, where the children of fallen soldiers were kept—and mistreated—after the war has been reported for ghostly sightings.

Are the tales true? Do the spirits of America's most terrible battle still roam the town of Gettysburg and the areas surrounding it? Many paranormal researchers have tried to find out. Investigators have recorded strange sounds and captured images that are difficult to explain. Does their work prove that the ghosts are real? Or are they just stories created out of the emotions and imaginations of those who have visited this historic battleground?

TIMELINE

1854—The Kansas-Nebraska Act is passed, allowing people in these territories to decide for themselves whether slavery should be legal. Prior to this act, slavery was outlawed in Kansas. Conflicts between pro-slavery and anti-slavery groups—and northern and southern states—become increasingly violent.

November 6, 1860—Abraham Lincoln is elected President of the United States.

December 20, 1860—South Carolina leaves the United States, becoming the first southern state to secede. Alabama, Georgia, Florida, Louisiana, Mississippi, Texas, Virginia, Arkansas, North Carolina, and Tennessee secede later, forming the Confederate States of America in February 1861.

April 11–13, 1861—Confederate troops demand control of Fort Sumter in South Carolina. They open fire on the fort on the morning of the 12th. This is the first battle of the Civil War. Union troops surrender the fort on the 13th.

July 21, 1861—The Battle of Bull Run (also known as the Battle of First Manassas) is fought.

November 6, 1861—Jefferson Davis is elected the president of the Confederate States of America.

April 6–7, 1862—The Battle of Shiloh takes place.

August 30–31, 1862—The Second Battle of Bull Run (or Second Manassas) is fought.

May 1–4, 1863—The Battle of Chancellorsville is fought; it is a Confederate victory but General Stonewall Jackson is mortally wounded.

July 1, 1863—Union and Confederate soldiers meet at the town of Gettysburg. The first shots are fired at about 7:30 a.m. Union troops are driven back to Cemetery Hill. Reinforcements for both sides arrive at Gettysburg throughout the night.

July 2, 1863—The Union holds Culp's Hill and Cemetery Hill, Little Round Top, and Devil's Den. Fighting takes place across Gettysburg throughout the day. Confederates attempt to capture Peach Orchard and Devil's Den, but are unable to drive out Union troops.

July 3, 1863—Fighting occurs for seven hours but there is no real progress on either side. Confederate General Robert E. Lee commands a frontal assault of 12,000 to 14,000 soldiers, later known as Pickett's Charge. They march across an open field as Union soldiers fire at them from behind stone walls. Huge casualties force the Confederates back.

November 23–25, 1863—The Battle of Chattanooga is fought. The Confederate army is defeated, retreating further into the south.

April 14, 1865—Abraham Lincoln is assassinated.

May 12, 1865—The final battle of the Civil War is fought. The war officially ends on June 2.

GLOSSARY

apparition (ap-uh-RISH-uhn)—the visible appearance of a ghost

artillery (ar-TIL-uh-ree)—cannons and other large guns used during battles

déjà vu (DEY-jah VOO)—the feeling that you have seen or experienced something before

deserter (di-ZURT-ure)—a military member who leaves duty without permission

forensics (FUH-ren-siks)—using science to help investigate or solve crimes; a forensic investigation uses fingerprints, blood tests, handwriting analysis, etc.

genealogy (GEE-nee-ohl-oh-gee)—the study of families and family history

hallucination (huh-loo-suh-NAY-shuhn)—something seen that is not really there

monument (MON-yuh-muhnt)—a statue or building that is meant to remind people of an event or a person

paranormal (pair-uh-NOR-muhl)—having to do with an unexplained event that has no scientific explanation

re-enactment (REE-uhn-akt-mehnt)—a performance of an old event, such as a theatrical performance, a

sacred (SAY-krid)—holy or having to do with religion

skirmish (SKUR-mish)—a minor fight in a battle

sniper (SNY-pur)—a soldier trained to shoot at long-distance targets from a hidden place

spirit orb (SPIHR-it ORB)—balls of light believed to contain peoples' spirits or souls

supernatural (soo-pur-NACH-ur-uhl)—something that cannot be given an ordinary explanation

OTHER PATHS TO EXPLORE

In this book you've seen how terrifying being alone in a haunted place can be. But haunted places can mean different things to different people. Seeing an experience from many points of view is an important part of understanding it.

Here are a few ideas for other haunted points of view to explore:

- "Brother against brother" is a common phrase associated with the Civil War. What would it be like to know a close family member was fighting for the opposite side?

- The Battle of Gettysburg was fought in and around the town. Soldiers ducked inside houses while townspeople hid in cellars and storerooms. Field hospitals were set up in shops and churches. Bodies piled up in the middle of town. What kind of fear might you have felt as a resident of Gettysburg?

- More than 620,000 soldiers lost their lives fighting in the Civil War. But for every three soldiers killed in battle, another five died of illness or injury. Imagine what living through the war might be like, without the medical care we are used to today.

READ MORE

Cordell, M. R. *Courageous Women of the Civil War: Soldiers, Spies, Medics, and More.* Chicago: Chicago Review Press, 2016.

Dunn, Joeming W. *Gettysburg.* Minneapolis: Graphic Planet, an imprint of Magic Wagon, 2016.

Roberts, Russell. *Gettysburg: History and Legend.* Kennett Square, Penn.: Purple Toad Publishing, 2015.

INTERNET SITES

Use FactHound to find Internet sites related to this book. All of the sites on FactHound have been researched by our staff.

Here's all you do:
Visit *www.facthound.com*
Type in this code: 9781515736493

INDEX